BEST. M♥M JOKES. EVER.

CHANTELLE GRACE

BroadStreet
PUBLISHING

BroadStreet Kids
Racine, Wisconsin, USA

BroadStreet Kids is an imprint of BroadStreet Publishing Group, LLC.
Broadstreetpublishing.com

BEST. MOM JOKES. EVER.

ISBN 978-1-4245-5644-1

Content compiled by Chantelle Grace.

Design by Chris Garborg | garborgdesign.com
Editorial services by Michelle Winger | literallyprecise.com
Cover and interior images from Bigstock (191708512, 191891476).

Printed in the United States of America.

18   19   20   21   22   23   24   7   6   5   4   3   2   1

Author Bio

CHANTELLE GRACE is a witty wordsmith who loves music, art, and competitive games. She is fascinated by God's intricate design of the human body. As she works her way through medical school, she knows it's important to share the gift of laughter with those around her. When she's not studying abroad, she makes her home in Prior Lake, Minnesota.

TABLE OF CONTENTS ....

QUESTIONS FOR MOM

Kid: Why did the chicken cross the road?

Mom: Ask your father.

Kid: Why are computers so smart?

Mom: Because they listen to their motherboards.

Kid: What is it?

Mom: It is a pronoun.

Kid: Is insecticide good for mosquitos?

Mom: No, it kills them.

Daughter: Who's the greatest daughter in the world?

> Mom: I don't know, you'll have to ask your grandmother.

Kid: Why is it so windy inside a sports arena?

> Mom: It's all those fans.

Kid: Why do we put candles on the top of a birthday cake?

> Mom: Because it's too hard to put them on the bottom.

Kid: Were any famous men or women born on my birthday?

> Mom: No, only babies.

Kid: Which hand is it better to write with?

> Mom: Neither. You should use a pen.

Kid: Mom, can you call Dad's phone? He lost it.

Mom: Dad's phone? Dad's phone?!

Kid: What do you call an old snowman?

Mom: Water.

Kid: Can I please see a butterfly?

Mom: Sure, just throw some butter out the window.

Kid: Do you know that sometimes I feel invisible?

Mom: Who said that?

Kid: Can I have a huge space party?

Mom: Sure, I'll planet.

Kid: Will the pizza be long?

Mom: No, it will be round.

Kid: Can I become a vegetarian?

Mom: *I think that would be a big missed steak.*

Kid: Can we have a dog for Christmas?

Mom: *No, we will have turkey like we usually do.*

Kid: Why did the farmer ride his horse into town?

Mom: *It would have been too heavy to carry.*

Kid: Do you like Jolly Ranchers?

Mom: *I prefer happy cowboys.*

Kid: What's your favorite Christmas Carol?

Mom: *Silent Night.*

Mom: You can't swim on a full stomach.

Kid: *What if I do the backstroke instead?*

Kid to Mom: I'm hungry. I'm tired. I'm thirsty. I'm hot. I can't find my shoes. Can I go to a friend's house?

Kid to Dad: Where's Mom?

AROUND THE HOUSE

After we painted my room, my mom said the room was cold.

She thinks it needs a second coat.

My mom said my room is so dusty...

the bugs ride around in dune buggies.

What is a mother's favorite time?

Bedtime.

What kind of shoes do mother ninjas lay out for their kids?

Sneakers.

What did the mama chimney say
to her son?

You're too young to smoke.

I set up my bed in our fireplace.

Now I sleep like a log.

Mom was talking about our ceiling
yesterday. She said she's not sure
if it's her favorite.

But it's definitely up there.

My mom must have done 2,000 pounds
of laundry.

*She always says she feels like she's
washing a ton.*

Mom: Did you take a bath?

Kid: Why, is one missing?

Mom: I think I'll go to that lamp party after all.

Kid: I heard it's going to be lit.

Cleaning the house fascinates everyone in my family.

They can sit and watch me for hours!

Today I saw that my ironing board cover was wrinkled.

I laughed at the irony.

Then I laughed again because irony has the word iron *in it.*

All of us have moments in our lives that test our courage.

Taking children into a house with white carpet is one of them.

Mom: Based on the amount of laundry I do each week...

I'm thinking there are more people living here that I haven't met yet.

Mom: I thought there was a spider on the floor, but it was just yarn.

It's dead yarn now.

IN THE KITCHEN

What do moms call a fake noodle?

An im-pasta.

What kind of snack does your mom serve during a scary movie?

Ice cream.

What kind of nuts have no shells?

Doughnuts.

What do you call 150 strawberries bunched together?

Strawberry jam.

What did the mayonnaise say to the mom who opened the fridge?

Close the door; I'm dressing.

What did the mama tomato say to the baby tomato?

Catch up!

Why did the mama cookie take her kid to the doctor?

Because it felt crumby.

What did the mama burger name her daughter?

Patty.

My mom says not to worry about broken tomatoes.

She can fix them with tomato paste.

Kid: This is a very average potato.

Mom: I think it must be a commentator.

Why did the mama banana take her kid
to the doctor?

Because it wasn't peeling well.

My mom gave me shoes made out
of banana peels.

She calls them slippers.

What did the baby corn say
to the mama corn?

Where is pop?

What are the two things your mom won't
let you have for breakfast?

Lunch and dinner.

What did the mama lemon give
to her sick kid?

Lemon-aid.

Where do hamburgers go to dance?

The meat-ball.

GO OUTSIDE!

What did the cloud's mother make him wear under his raincoat?

Thunderwear.

I told my mom that there is a pot of gold at the end of a rainbow.

She said that's silly; the letter w is at the end of rainbow.

What is the most frustrating thing about being a tree?

Having so many limbs and not being able to walk.

What did the volcano say to his mom?

I lava you so much.

What did the ocean say when it saw the Queen Mother coming?

Nothing, it just waved.

What does the mama snowman give her children for breakfast?

Frosted flakes.

What does a mama scarecrow give her kids for snack?

Straw berries.

What washes up on very small beaches?

Microwaves.

What did the trees wear to Mother Nature's pool party?

Swimming trunks!

Where do saplings go to learn?

Elementree school.

What do you call an attractive volcano?

Lava-ble.

Kid: Can you help me identify this weeping tree?

Mom: Yes, but you willow me one.

What did the big flower say to the little flower?

Hey, bud.

I asked my mom for a brief explanation of an acorn.

She said, in a nutshell, it's an oak tree.

Kid: How should I keep warm
in a cold room?

Mom: Go to the corner.
It's always ninety degrees.

Kid: How can I tell if it's cold outside?

Mom: Go outside.

My mom always says if the WiFi isn't
working...

it's probably God's way of telling me
I should go outside.

ANIMAL MAMAS

How does a mama penguin make pancakes?

With her flippers.

How do bears keep cool in the summer?

They use bear conditioning.

What did the mama dog make for her kid's birthday?

Pupcakes.

Mama bear: Teddy, you need to eat all of your dinner.

Teddy bear: I can't, Mama, I'm stuffed.

What do mama birds give their sick chicks?

A tweetment.

How does a mama chicken bake a cake?

From scratch.

What did the mama pig give her sick baby pig?

Oink-ment.

What did the mama duck say to the daddy duck?

You quack me up.

What subject did the mama snake teach her children first?

Hiss-tory.

What did the mama buffalo say to her kid when she dropped him off at school?

Bi-son.

We saw an alligator wearing a vest the other day.

Mom said it must have been an investigator.

How do bees get to school?

In the school buzz.

I asked my mom for a milk shake.

She told me to put our cow on the trampoline.

MOM'S FAVORITE PUNS

What did one toilet say to the other?

You look flushed.

How many skunks does it take
to stink up a house?

A phew.

To the guy who invented zero:

Thanks for nothing.

There's a new pillow out.

It's making headlines.

Why did the mama drum make the baby drum take a nap?

It was beat.

What does a frog say when it washes a window?

Rub it, rub it, rub it.

How did the mom get the egg up the mountain?

She had it scrambled up.

What is Irish and left outside all summer?

Paddy O'Furniture.

How does a penguin build its house?

Igloos it together.

What did the quilt say to the bed?

I have you covered.

Why did the tired mom run around
her bed?

To catch up on some sleep.

Why did the mom write on the window?

To make a lesson very clear.

What do you do if your mom rolls
her eyes at you?

Pick them up and roll them back.

Why did the mom go outside
with her purse open?

*She was expecting some change
in the weather.*

Someone stole all my lamps.

I couldn't be more delighted.

Mom says I should never wear
a cardboard belt.

It would be a waist of paper.

Why couldn't the mama pirate play cards?

Because she was sitting on the deck.

Where did the mama frog ask her kids to leave their hats and coats?

In the croak-room.

Someone stole my special mug.

I have no pi-tea for the guy.

I was trying to catch some fog earlier.

I mist.

I value toilet paper.

It plays an important role in my life.

I'd love to know how the earth rotates.

It would totally make my day.

I'd like to thank my arms...

for always being at my side.

I was so excited when spring finally arrived.

I wet my plants.

MY MOM TOLD ME

My mom said the biggest problem with snow boots...

is that they melt.

My mom told me to eat like a train.

Chew, chew.

Mom said if I eat shoe polish and yeast...

everyday, I will rise and shine.

Mom always told me to be careful. She talked about the kidnapping in the park.

They woke him up.

My mom got pretty mad at the Italian restaurant last week.

She gave the chef a pizza her mind.

Mom said she wouldn't eat at a restaurant on the moon.

She wouldn't like the atmosphere.

My mom told me to stay away from my brother's cheese.

She said it's nacho cheese.

Mom said I shouldn't tell secrets on the farm.

Apparently the potatoes have eyes and the corn has ears.

My mom told me she feels like an elevator.

She thinks she's coming down with something.

Mom says Peter Pan flies around
all the time.

He never lands.

Mom told me I should get a job
in a bakery.

Then I could just loaf around.

Mom says I shouldn't trust atoms.

They make up everything.

Mom told me my nose is in the middle
of my face because...

it is the scenter.

My mom told me moon rocks taste much
better than earth rocks.

They are meteor.

Mom looked into the sky tonight and told me the moon had enough to eat.

She could tell because it was full.

My mom says we are like two pennies.

Together we make cents.

My mom told me if I want to watch a tissue dance...

I need to put a little boogie in it.

I wanted to buy shoes with Velcro...

but my mom said that was just a big rip off.

My mom says of all the dogs, a hot dog is the most noble.

It feeds the hand that bites it.

Mom said my socks are too holey.

I can only wear them to church.

Vegans believe meat eaters and butchers are gross.

> But my mom says those who sell you fruits and vegetables are grocer.

Every time my mom leaves cookies in the oven too long she says,

> "These are Darth Vader cookies. They're a little on the dark side."

Every time we go to the ocean, my mom tells me to say hello.

> The ocean just waves back.

I thought my mom was constantly laughing at me because she ends all of her texts with **LOL**.

> Then I found out she thought she was sending lots of love.

My mom told me to brush my teeth and get ready for bed in her "mom voice."

The neighbors also brushed their teeth and got in bed.

My mom told me to follow my dreams,

so I went back to bed.

KNOCK-KNOCK JOKES

Knock knock.

Who's there?

Doughnut.

Doughnut who?

Doughnut ask; it's a secret.

Knock knock.

Who's there?

Broccoli.

Broccoli who?

Broccoli doesn't have a last name, silly.

Knock knock.

Who's there?

Dishes.

Dishes who?

Dishes me. Who are you?

Knock knock.

Who's there?

Cash.

Cash who?

I knew you were a nut.

Knock knock.

Who's there?

Figs.

Figs who?

Figs the doorbell; it's broken.

Knock knock.

Who's there?

Banana.

Banana who?

Knock knock.

Who's there?

Banana.

Banana who?

Knock knock.

Who's there?

Banana.

Banana who?

Knock knock.

Who's there?

Orange.

Orange who?

Orange you glad I didn't say banana?

Knock knock.

Who's there?

Isadora.

Isadora who?

Isadora really so hard to open?

Knock knock.

Who's there?

Olive.

Olive who?

Olive you.

Knock knock.

Who's there?

Noah.

Noah who?

*Noah good place to get
something to eat?*

Knock knock.

Who's there?

Mikey.

Mikey who?

Mikey doesn't work. Let me in.

Knock knock.

Who's there?

Luke.

Luke who?

Luke through the peep hole and you'll see.

Knock knock.

Who's there?

Justin.

Justin who?

Justin time for dinner.

Knock knock.

Who's there?

Lettuce.

Lettuce who?

Lettuce in; it's cold out here!

Knock knock.

Who's there?

Claire.

Claire who?

Claire the way; I'm coming through!

Knock knock.

Who's there?

Cow says.

Cow says who?

No, silly! A cow says Mooooo!

Knock knock.

Who's there?

Canoe.

Canoe who?

Canoe let me in please?

Knock knock.

Who's there?

Wooden shoe.

Wooden shoe who?

Wooden shoe like to let me in?

Knock knock.

Who's there?

Dishes.

Dishes who?

Dishes a nice place you've got here!

Knock knock.

Who's there?

Sadie.

Sadie who?

Sadie magic word and I'll disappear.

Knock knock.

Who's there?

Pizza.

Pizza who?

Pizza really great guy.
You should let him in.

Knock knock.

Who's there?

Leaf.

Leaf who?

Leaf the door unlocked so I can get in.

Knock knock.

Who's there?

Ken.

Ken who?

Ken someone let me in please?

Knock knock.

Who's there?

Alpaca.

Alpaca who?

Alpaca the suitcase; you pack the trunk.

Knock knock.

Who's there?

Atch.

Atch who?

Bless you!

Knock knock.

Who's there?

Interrupting cow.

Interrupt...

Moo!

Knock knock.

Who's there?

Juno.

Juno who?

Juno how to open the door?
It's locked.

Knock knock.

Who's there?

Dozen.

Dozen who?

Dozen anyone want to let me in?

MOMS AT WORK

My mom is a math teacher.

Her favorite dessert is pi.

My mom used to be a doughnut maker.

*She said she got sick
of the hole business.*

My mom is an astronaut.

She eats at launch time.

My mom is a lawyer.

She wears lawsuits to work.

My mom is an orthodontist.

She braces herself during an
earthquake.

I think my mom must be a doctor.

She keeps asking for more patients.

My mom always told me not to be quick
about finding faults.

She's a great woman,
but a terrible geologist.

My mom used to work in the bank.

Then she lost interest.

My mom sells broken puppets.

No strings attached.

My mom quit her job working for Nike.

She just couldn't do it anymore.

My mom is a maze designer.

She gets completely lost in her work.

My mom is a bug sorter.

She boxes all the right ticks.

My mom wanted to be a deli worker.

Any way she sliced it, she couldn't cut the mustard.

My mom was a professional fisher.

Then she discovered she couldn't live on her net income.

My mom was a seamstress until she figured out she wasn't suited for it.

It was a so-so job.

SPORTS MOMS

What's the difference between a hockey mom and a Pitbull?

Lipstick.

What is a cheerleader's favorite color?

Yeller.

Why can't Cinderella play soccer?

She's always running away from the ball.

When is a baby good at basketball?

When he's dribbling.

What lights up in a soccer stadium?

A soccer match.

What's a banker's favorite gymnastic event?

The vault.

Where do moms go to buy sports uniforms?

New Jersey.

What do referees send during the holidays?

Yellow cards.

Mom says I should really try to reach goals.

Then I would be a successful forward.

Why is baseball a mom's favorite sport?

Because it's played on a diamond.

Why do soccer players do well in school?

They know how to use their heads.

Why do volleyball players make extra money?

It's common practice to tip a good server.

Why do gymnasts make the best friends?

They're always bending over backwards.

How did the swim team get enough money for their road trip to Nationals?

They pooled their resources.

How is playing the bagpipes like throwing a javelin blindfolded?

You don't have to be very good to get people's attention.

Kid: I don't really see the point in archery.

Mom: You would if one of the arrows flew toward you.

Since I quit hockey...

I've lost the goal in my life.

My skiing skills are getting worse.

They're really going downhill fast.

I think there are about 1-2 million baseball fields in the world.

But that's just a ballpark number.

My tennis opponent wasn't very happy with my serve.

He kept returning it.

Why can't tennis players ever find happiness?

Love means nothing to them.

I just burned 2000 calories.

*That's the last time I leave the
brownies in the oven while I nap.*

I named my dog 6 Miles...

so I can tell people I walk 6 Miles every day.

HELP ME WITH MY HOMEWORK!

I told my mom I couldn't reach the high notes in my choir class.

She said I should get a ladder.

I told my mom it was hard to get straight A's.

She said I should use a ruler.

What did the mama elf teach her kids before they went to school?

The elfabet.

My mom doesn't like math very much.

She says it has too many problems.

My mom sent me to Sundae School.

She was hoping I'd learn how to make banana splits.

Mom: What did you learn in school today?

Kid: Not enough. I have to go back tomorrow.

Mom: Why did you eat your homework?

Kid: You said it was a piece of cake.

Don't do your math homework in the jungle.

If you add 4+4, you get ate.

What did the fishing rod say to the boat?

Canoe help me with my homework?

Ever since I took geometry at school...

my life has turned around 360 degrees.

Mom: Draw me a picture of a house.

Kid: Is that my homework?

Kid: Will I get into trouble
for something I haven't done?

Mom: No, why?

*Kid: Because I haven't done my
homework.*

Child: Why do magicians do so well
in school?

Mom: They're good at trick questions.

MOMS RULE

Mom: I'm standing outside.

In other words, I'm outstanding.

There's a legend that if you go take a shower and scream "MOM!" three times...

a nice lady appears with the towel you forgot.

Mom, talking to her house: We can't both look good at the same time.

It's either you or me.

If at first you don't succeed,

try it the way your mom told you to do it in the beginning.

Mom: I spent my day in a well.

I would say that's a day well spent.

What are the only laundry instructions that make sense?

Give it to your mother.

Whenever I can't find something in my room, I look for it under everything.

But mostly I yell for my mom.

Some moms can do everything.

I think I should get them to do some things for me.

If moms are told to sleep
when the baby sleeps,

*then should they clean when the baby
cleans, or cook when the baby cooks?*

Mom: Don't text me for the next hour.
I'm on the treadmill.

Kid: I wasn't planning on it.

Mom: What did I just say?

IN THE BIBLE

Did Adam and Eve ever have a date?

No, but they did have an apple.

Where was Solomon's temple located?

On the side of his head.

Where is the first tennis match mentioned in the Bible?

When Joseph served in Pharaoh's court.

What did Adam say to his wife on the day before Christmas?

It's Christmas, Eve!

How does Moses make his coffee?

Hebrews it.

On the Ark, Noah probably got milk from the cows. What did he get from the ducks?

Quackers.

Why didn't Noah go fishing?

Because he only had two worms.

Who was the smartest man in the Bible?

Abraham. He knew a Lot.

Who was the fastest runner in the Bible?

Adam, because he was first in the human race.

Why did the unemployed man get excited while looking through his Bible?

He thought he saw a job.

What animal could Noah not trust?

The cheetah.

Who was the greatest comedian
in the Bible?

Samson. He brought the house down.

What kind of man was Boaz
before he married?

Ruthless.

Which Bible character is a locksmith?

Zac-key-us.

Which Bible character had no parents?

Joshua, son of Nun.

Where is the first baseball game
in the Bible?

Genesis. "In the big inning..."

COULD YOU BE A MOM?

Smear peanut butter on the couch and place a fish stick under the cushions. Leave it all there for a month. If it doesn't bother you, *you could be a mom.*

If you love arguing about why it's important to wear a coat when it's 12 degrees outside, *you could be a mom.*

Buy a 55 gallon drum of Legos and spread them on the floor. Put on a blindfold and walk barefoot through your house. If you have no problem with this, *you could be a mom.*

Buy an unhappy octopus and dress it. Then put a shoe on a potato. If you succeed, *you could be a mom.*

Take two small animals to the grocery store with you. Goats are best. Pay for any damage they cause in the store. If you are okay with this, *you could be a mom.*

Fill a bag with ten pounds of sand. Wet it thoroughly. Rock and hum with the bag until 9:00pm. Lay it down and set your alarm for 10:00pm. Get up, pick up the bag and sing every song you know. You will need enough songs to get you through to 4:00am. Set your alarm for 5:00am. Get up and make breakfast. Do this for about two years and make sure you look happy. If you can survive this, *you could be a mom.*

Attach a large beanbag to the front of your clothes. Leave it there for nine months. Remove ten of the beans. If you find this enjoyable, *you could be a mom.*

Suspend a half-full milk jug from the ceiling. As it is moving, try to shove spoons of cereal in the mouth of the jug. Pretend to be an airplane while you are doing this. Now pour the contents of the jug on the floor. If you find this entertaining, *you could be a mom.*

Fish an old toy out of the toilet. Immediately throw it down the sink drain and retrieve it again. If you can do this without gagging, *you could be a mom.*

If you talk back to Dora when she asks a question on TV because you feel like it's more awkward to sit in silence while she stares at you, *you could be a mom.*

YOU ARE A MOM IF...

You double-knot everything you tie.

You hum the Barney song when you do the dishes.

You automatically rock back and forth when you hear a baby cry.

You can never go to the bathroom alone, and typically someone is screaming outside the door.

You don't mind the smell of strained carrots mixed with applesauce.

You sob during the scene in Dumbo where the mom is taken away, and you can't even watch Bambi anymore.

Your idea of a good day is one in which none of your children spills (or leaks) anything on you.

You understand Klingon.

You spend an hour looking for the
sunglasses that are sitting on your head.

Your feet stick to the kitchen floor
and you don't care.

You will suck the dirt off a pacifier that
has just hit the floor in order to keep
your baby happy.

Gourmet cooking includes making
Rice Krispies bars.

Your favorite smell is fresh linen followed closely by baby shampoo.

A crusty face won't stop you kissing it.

You do the work of twenty, for free.

You are the best maid on the planet, because you clean all day.

You can make meals every day, for at least 18 years.

You get questioned more than
an interviewee.

Your go-to answer is, "Because I said so."

You are okay making dinner and then
sweeping 90% of it off the floor.

You make excuses to carry wet wipes
in your purse even if your kids aren't
with you.

You consider Goldfish crackers
a food group.

You wish there was a drive through
for everything.

You do more in seven minutes than a lot
of people can do in a day.

Instead of running away from vomit,
you run toward it.

Going to the grocery store by yourself
is a luxury.

You have a secret stash of chocolate
because you're sick of sharing.

You wake up in your kid's bed without knowing how you got there.

You have been out in public with a superhero band-aid around your finger.

You think you can cut hair.

THINGS YOU WILL NEVER HEAR YOUR MOM SAY

"Go ahead and keep that stray dog. I'll be happy to feed and walk it every day."

"If Johnny's mom said it's ok, well then, it's fine with me."

"Curfew is just a general time to shoot for. I like waiting up until you get home."

"Please leave all the lights on. It makes the house bright and cheery."

"How can you see the TV from that far away?"

"Please call me from your cell phone when you are downstairs. I like phone communication better than real conversations."

"I used to skip school a lot, too."

"If you need me, just yell. A hundred times, please."

"Your shirt is really the best napkin."

"You probably won't need a jacket in the snow today."

"Please stop helping me do the dishes. I like doing them by myself after I have prepared your meal."

"Did you say you are bored? Let's find something really fun for you to do! Maybe you could play more video games, or get back on your phone!"

"I prefer to clean the house when my kids are home."

"Don't worry about eating your vegetables. Just eat the food on your plate that you like."

"I prefer you to answer, 'I don't know' to all of my questions."

"Beds are really for jumping on."

"I told you, life is always fair."

"You should keep making that face. Nothing will happen."

"Don't wait until your father gets home. Let's talk about this now."

"What matters the most is who started it."

"Please touch that."

"I like it best when you bother me while I'm on the phone."

"Don't worry about washing your hands. They will just get dirty again anyway."

"You should wait until bedtime to start your homework."

"Let's see how much water you can transfer from the bathtub to the floor."

"If I don't come find you immediately after you yell for me, please keep shouting my name."

"I am your maid. At your service."

"Doesn't that puddle look fun to jump in?"

"I prefer my dinner cold."

"I wish I could keep all of your artwork on my fridge."

MOM MYTHS

"If you swallow a watermelon seed,
the fruit will grow in your stomach."

"Cracking your knuckles causes arthritis."

"Reading in the dark will hurt your eyes."

"Going outside with wet hair
will give you a cold."

"Swimming after eating causes cramps."

"Eat your crusts and your hair will be curly."

"If you keep crossing your eyes,
they will get stuck."

"Once you start shaving your legs,
the hair will grow back thicker."

"Eating sugar at bedtime
will keep you up at night."

"It takes seven years
to digest swallowed gum."

"Milk is bad for you when you have a cold."

"Carrots improve your vision."

"Pruney fingers means it's time
to get out of the water."

"Letting your wounds breathe helps them
heal faster."

"Rusty nails are worse to step on."

"Soda will settle your stomach."

"Feed a cold; starve a fever."

"Storing batteries in the freezer will help prolong battery life."

FAMOUS MOM QUOTES

Paul Revere's mother:

I don't care where you think you have to go, young man.

Midnight is past your curfew.

Michelangelo's mother:

Mike, can't you paint on walls like other children?

Do you have any idea how hard it is to get that stuff off the ceiling?

Mona Lisa's mother:

After all that money your father and I spent on braces, Mona,

that's the biggest smile you can give us?

Abraham Lincoln's mother:

Again with the stovepipe hat, Abe?

Can't you just wear a baseball cap like the other kids?

Goldilocks' mother:

I've got a bill here for a busted chair from the Bear family.

You know anything about this, Goldie?

Albert Einstein's mother:

Albert, it's your senior picture.

Can't you do something about your hair?

Gel, hairspray... anything?

Humpty Dumpty's mother:

If I've told you once,

I've told you a thousand times not to sit on that wall!

But would you listen? Noooo!

Batman's mother:

It's a nice car, Bruce,

but do you realize how much the insurance is going to be?

Superman's mother:

Clark, your father and I have discussed it,

and we've decided you can have your own phone.

Now will you quit spending so much time in all those phone booths?

Barney's mother:

I realize strained plums are your favorite, Barney,

but you're starting to look a little purple.

Mary's mother:

I'm not upset that your lamb followed you to school, Mary,

but I would like to know how he got a better grade than you.

Little Miss Muffet's mother:

Well, all I've got to say is if you don't get off your tuffet

and start cleaning your room,

there will be a lot more spiders around here.

Jonah's mother:

That's a nice story, Jonah,

but now really tell me where you have been for the last three days.

Thomas Edison's mother:

Of course I'm proud that you invented the electric light bulb, Thomas.

Now turn that light off and go to bed!